Art and self-expression are what hip-hop culture is all about.

Parts of hip-hop

Hip-hop culture consists of four major parts: the DJ, the MC, graffiti, and break-dancing. Each part of hip-hop is an art form. All types of hip-hop artist are constantly trying to be the best. This is good for hip-hop. It means that the artists are always inventing new styles. This book mostly focuses on the music side of hip-hop – the DJs and MCs.

What is hip-hop?

There are many things that go into making a hip-hop song. It starts with energetic music played by a disc jockey (**DJ**). The DJ usually plays two vinyl records at the same time. He or she spins these records on two **turntables** (record players). The turntables are connected to a mixer. This allows the DJ to **mix** records. Mixing means the DJ slides a switch back and forth to play music from each turntable on its own, or both at the same time. Modern DJs also use computers, drum machines (electronic devices that sound like drums), **synthesizers** (keyboard-like instruments), and other devices to create music.

The master of ceremonies (**MC**) **raps** over the beat of the music. To rap is to make rhymes with words, like reciting a poem. An MC often has a gift for using words, creating thoughtful **lyrics** and clever rhymes.

Rap or hip-hop?

The words *rap* and *hip-hop* are often thought to mean the same thing. Rap refers to lyrics said or rapped by an MC. Hip-hop refers to the **culture** as a whole. Rap is a part of hip-hop culture.

An MC and DJ work together to create hip-hop music.

Learning to be a DJ requires a lot of practice. It is like learning to play an instrument.

Other players

A band can also be used to create hip-hop music. The Roots are a hip-hop band. They use instruments to make music that sounds like a hip-hop DJ.

Some hip-hop artists are **beat-boxers**. Beat-boxers use their tongues, mouths, lips, and voices to create a beat. US rapper Doug E. Fresh never even had a DJ or band. He did everything with his mouth. Biz Markie was also well known for his beat-boxing abilities.

Multiple MCs

Many hip-hop groups have more than one MC. Some of these groups include:
Grandmaster Flash and the Furious Five
Wu-Tang Clan
Jurassic 5
Run-DMC
Beastie Boys
De La Soul
A Tribe Called Quest.

Write and sing your own rap

Creating hip-hop music involves hard work and practice. Listening, writing, and reading are important skills in rapping. They are part of the creative process that goes into rapping.

Steps to follow:

1. Listen to a few hip-hop songs for ideas. Try "Rapper's Delight" by the Sugarhill Gang. Hip-hop artists often listen to other music and musicians to find their own ideas. Pay attention to how the MCs rhyme. They might rap smoothly or in a choppy way.

2. Pick six words that rhyme.

3. Put each word in a sentence so that it is like a story. Use a dictionary, thesaurus, or rhyming dictionary if you need help.

4. Rap your new lyrics to a hip-hop song or create a new beat for your rap. Have a friend try to beat-box by making noises with his or her mouth as you rap. You can both tap your feet or clap your hands.

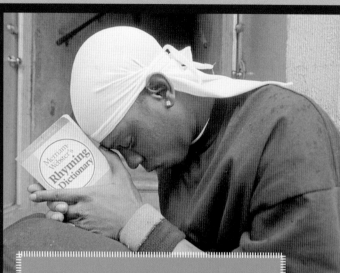

Spending time experimenting with and learning new words is how hip-hop artists (like Yykkes, shown here) become great.

Tools of the trade

You can use a dictionary to look up words you do not know. Also try using a thesaurus. It will give you lists of words that mean the same or the opposite of a particular word. A rhyming dictionary will give you lists of rhyming words.

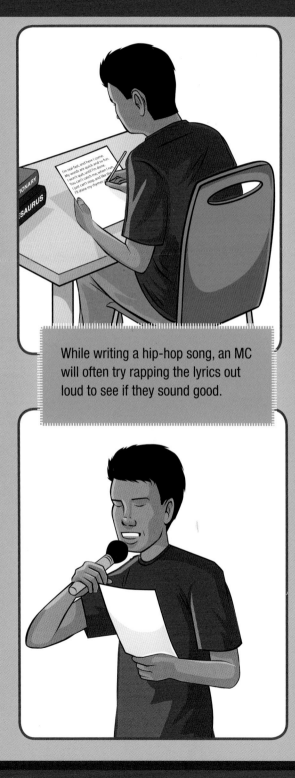

While writing a hip-hop song, an MC will often try rapping the lyrics out loud to see if they sound good.

5. Rap your lyrics out loud to yourself or your friends.

6. Repeat the process to create several short raps or a whole song.

Example

I'm real fast, and here I come.

My words are quick and so fun.

I won't quit, until I'm done.

You can't catch me, when I run.

I just can't stop, and like the sun,

I'll shine my rhymes on everyone!

History in the making

Hip-hop began in the early 1970s in poor African-American and Afro-Caribbean neighbourhoods in New York City, USA. **DJs** would play at gatherings and parties held in the streets and public parks. They would plug a sound system into a streetlight's power source to play music.

Hey, DJ – play that song!

Hip-hop first received attention in 1973. At that time, Jamaican-born DJ Kool Herc stood out among other DJs. He started to extend the "break" of songs. This is the part of a song that occurs somewhere between the middle and end. At this point there is no singing and a drumbeat takes over. Herc extended the break of songs by using two copies of the same record and cutting back and forth, creating what is known as a **break beat**.

DJ Kool Herc began his career DJing at block parties and in parks.

By the mid- to late 1970s, people started to notice other DJs who used Herc's style. One was Afrika Bambaataa, who led a tough street gang. In time, Bambaataa would convert his gang into the Zulu Nation. This is a group dedicated to peace, unity, harmony, and hip-hop. The Zulu Nation helped to bring hip-hop to Europe.

Grandmaster Flash would become more popular than Herc because of his skill and speed at spinning records (see box below right). Grandmaster Flash and his group, the Furious Five, led the way in **MCing** and **freestyle rapping** competitions (see box below).

Afrika Bambaataa became known as the "Master of Records". This was because of his huge collection of records.

Competitive hip-hop

Some MCs compete in freestyle and battle raps on stage, or even on the street, to verbally prove who is more skilled. Freestyle rapping is rapping without preparing first. Battle rapping is attacking another MC with freestyle bragging and boasting raps.

"Who's spinning tonight?"

DJs spin records on **turntables**. So, "spinning" is another name for DJing.

Beyond the streets

In 1979 hip-hop went **mainstream**, meaning many people became aware of it. The song "Rapper's Delight" is thought to be the first song that popularised hip-hop. It was by a little-known group called the Sugarhill Gang from New Jersey, USA. Early DJs, such as Herc, Bambaataa, and Flash, had once been upset that their music was not being played on the radio. Now hip-hop had finally managed to announce itself to the world.

Sampling music

Sampling is when DJs or **producers** (people who direct the recording process) use a turntable, computer, or tape player to extract (pull out or copy) part of a song. They might extract a catchy beat or break. This part of the song is then taken, or sampled, and used in a new song.

Record hunting

DJs are highly competitive. In order to be different and have the best music, they spend a lot of time looking for uncommon records and sounds. DJs also look for two copies of the same record in order to create the break beat.

A DJ will visit many different record shops, resale shops, and even car boot sales looking for records to try.

Run-DMC had two MCs, DMC and Run (left and middle in this photo). A DJ called Jam-Master Jay (on the right) was the third member.

"Old School" and "New School"

Original hip-hop produced between the mid-1970s to the early 1980s is generally considered "Old School". The sounds of Run-DMC, which first hit the scene in 1983, are "Old School". LL Cool J and many others followed. These new sounds are considered "New School".

The group Run-DMC became popular in 1983. Their sound featured rapping with rhyming **lyrics**. It had little backing music other than heavy drumbeats. Until that time, hip-hop audiences had mostly heard a dance beat.

The Beastie Boys are a three-man group from New York City, USA. In 1986 they became the first popular white hip-hop act in the United States. Their youthful and clever rapping style made them a popular mainstream group. They helped to make hip-hop familiar to white audiences around the world.

13

Break-dancers try daring moves such as head spins.

Music is a major part of hip-hop **culture**. But from its early history, art forms such as **break-dancing** and **graffiti** have also made important contributions to hip-hop.

Break-dancing

During the early days of hip-hop, dancers who would dance during the "break" of a song became known as break boys or break girls, or "b-boys" and "b-girls". In 1977 a famous group of breakers, the Rock Steady Crew, formed. They helped make the dancing style popular. Today, break boys and break girls dance at competitions, parties, or even on the streets.

Graffiti

The first graffiti art was big, colourful, and competitive. In this way, it was just like other parts of hip-hop culture. Graffiti artists used highlighted outlines and wild designs. But graffiti that is spray-painted on walls of people's property is an act of **vandalism**. It is illegal. Some graffiti artists went from making illegal artwork to having their art shown in galleries.

Create a basic hip-hop dance

Break-dancing is an **improvisational** way to dance. This means you have to be able to perform without preparing ahead of time. "Top rocking" is moving the arms while the body remains in an upright position. Using the ground to complete moves such as spins, flips, and other leg movements is called "floor rocking". Try creating your own hip-hop dance.

Steps to follow:

1. Start with your feet together.

2. Slide your right foot away from your left foot.

3. Slide your left foot back next to your right.

4. Clap your hands.

5. Repeat the process going the opposite way.

6. Add the movement of nodding your head up and down.

7. Don't be afraid to try some dance moves, too. Try spinning around in a circle on your feet or your back.

8. Practise your new dance routine.

9. Turn on a hip-hop song and perform your dance for others.

Hip-hop is about creativity. People can make up their own new dance moves and blend them together with old ones.

15

Hip-hop artists

Hip-hop artists and styles in the United States today are classified (sorted) into territories: the East Coast, West Coast, Midwest, and South.

Hip-hop territories

East Coast hip-hop music is typically known for its well-spoken **lyrics** about **urban** (city) life. It is also known for irregular, powerful beats.

West Coast hip-hop became known for "gangsta **rap**". This style of hip-hop uses slow, intense rhymes about gangs and violence. It uses smooth, regular beats.

The style of Midwestern hip-hop has been heavily influenced by all forms of hip-hop. There is nothing typical about Midwestern hip-hop. Few hip-hop artists from the Midwest share the same sound.

The music of Southern hip-hop, also known as "Dirty South", has an upbeat style that uses mostly simple and fun lyrics.

Different parts of the United States have unique styles of hip-hop.

Styles of hip-hop

Artists today create many types of hip-hop music. One type is about learning, problems in the world, and sometimes religion. Common, A Tribe Called Quest, De La Soul, and Mos Def are a few hip-hop artists who make this style of music.

Other artists create a type of hip-hop that is concerned with government. It also encourages listeners to explore different ideas and thoughts. Public Enemy was one of the first well-known hip-hop groups to use this style.

Mainstream and underground

Mainstream is music that receives a lot of attention from media such as newspapers, magazines, and television. It is often created to sell albums and make money. **Underground** hip-hop artists are those outside the mainstream. The lyrics of underground artists are often more respected than those of the mainstream. They usually focus on more mature and thoughtful topics. Some underground hip-hop groups move into the mainstream. Two popular underground artists are MF Doom and Cool Kids.

Cool Kids are a popular underground group from the Midwest.

Hip-hop stars

Many different artists have come out of the four hip-hop territories in the United States. The next few pages highlight just a small number of them.

East Coast

Jay-Z is from Brooklyn, New York, USA. He became a street **hustler** when he was a child, getting involved in questionable activities. Later he created his own record label, named Roc-A-Fella Records, to start his own hip-hop career. His first album, *Reasonable Doubt*, was released in 1996. In 2004 Jay-Z became president of Def Jam Records. He is one of the most successful hip-hop artists ever.

Nas is also from New York. As a young man he read many books and wrote short stories and poetry. His **gritty** (tough) and intelligent rhymes brought him fame and success. His first album, *Illmatic*, was released in 1994. It is in the East Coast style.

Jay-Z helped start a clothing company called Rocawear.

Nas began as an underground rapper in New York City.

Lauryn Hill is one of the most respected female hip-hop artists.

Dr. Dre has been at the centre of hip-hop since the early 1980s.

Lauryn Hill is from New Jersey, USA. As a teenager, Hill sang on the television programme *Showtime at the Apollo*. She also had a role on the soap opera *As the World Turns*. In secondary school she formed the band the Fugees with two of her friends. Their second album, *The Score*, released in 1996, won many awards. Her solo album *Miseducation of Lauryn Hill*, released in 1998, was a global success.

West Coast

Dr. Dre is from Los Angeles, California. He played a part in the creation of the "gangsta rap" style. Dr. Dre helped form Death Row Records in 1991. He combined booming beats along with **funk** music to create the "G-Funk" style. Funk is bass-heavy music characterised by **improvisation** (performing without preparing), horns, and strong **rhythms**. He is a successful music **producer** and has helped to create hits for artists such as Snoop Dogg, 50 Cent, Eve, the Game, and Young Buck.

West Coast underground

The following are some important West Coast underground artists:
Freestyle Fellowship
Pharcyde
Souls of Mischief
Hieroglyphics
Dilated Peoples
People Under the Stairs.

Midwest

Kanye West is from Chicago, USA. He left college to pursue a hip-hop career. He began producing songs for Chicago artists. Later, he produced music for Nas and Jay-Z. West released his first album, *The College Dropout*, in 2004. He has had great success creating his own new music and producing for others.

Kanye West is known for his bold fashion choices and attitude.

Eminem was born in Kansas City, Missouri, USA. In 1997 he took second place in a **freestyle** battle rap contest (see page 11) in Los Angeles, California. Dr. Dre took notice and added Eminem to his record label. Eminem became a popular underground rapper. After his *Slim Shady* album was released in 1999, he became one of the best-selling rappers of all time.

Eminem starred in a film based on his life called *8 Mile*.

André 3000 and Big Boi have also pursued acting careers.

South

OutKast are from Atlanta, Georgia. André 3000 and Big Boi went to secondary school together and were rival rappers until 1992, when the two formed OutKast. They released *Southernplayalisticadillacmuzik* in 1994. Their clever lyrics and smooth songs helped to define the Southern hip-hop style.

Lil Wayne is from New Orleans, Louisiana. He joined the rap group Hot Boys when he was a teenager. He helped form the record label Cash Money Records. From 2003 until 2008, he became famous by releasing **mixtapes**. These are CDs of an artist's music that are given out for free to attract fans. Lil Wayne has gone on to record music with many artists. He has worked on over 100 different music projects!

Lil Wayne has a unique-sounding voice and wild lyrics.

The business

Successful hip-hop artists make a lot of money recording music. Record companies and other industries have also realized they can make money from hip-hop. Some hip-hop artists have started their own record companies. Others have created fashion, film, and television careers linked to hip-hop.

The record business

The first hip-hop artists created a new sound and style because they loved the music. In time, hip-hop artists began to make money from their music. Making money by doing something they loved became a dream for many hip-hop artists. When an artist signs a record deal, he or she can make a lot of money.

Getting signed

Becoming "signed" to a record label is a long process. First, you have to be able to make music that people like. Musicians often practise for many years before even playing in front of an audience. They make recordings to give to record labels. The record labels listen to their music before deciding whether or not to help them make a record.

Def Jam

Russell Simmons and Rick Rubin started the first major hip-hop record label while they were at New York University. Def Jam would go on to launch the careers of Run-DMC, the Beastie Boys, LL Cool J, Public Enemy, and many other hip-hop artists.

Russell Simmons is a leading figure in the business of hip-hop.

Make a hip-hop poster

Record companies create posters to tell fans about hip-hop music and concerts. Use words, pictures, drawings, and colour to create a poster of your favourite hip-hop artist. You could also create one for your own hip-hop group.

Steps to follow:

1. Decide what your poster will tell others about: a group, a new album, or a concert?

2. Picture in your head what you want the poster to look like. What words will it use? What pictures will you use?

3. Use solid colours to draw pictures and use big, bubbly words (see the sample poster at right).

4. Use a dark colour to outline all the words and pictures.

5. Use other colours to add detail to the poster.

6. Display your poster for others to see.

As you make your poster, listen to the music and let it inspire you to create something great.

Beats, boasts, and beyond

The world of hip-hop is constantly changing. In the early 21st century, many hip-hop artists focused on glamour and wealth. Sean Combs, also known as "Puff Daddy", "P-Diddy", and "Diddy", played a major role in glamorising hip-hop with flashy songs. He **sampled** catchy music in party songs. He **rapped** about the "bling-bling" style of expensive things such as jewellery and cars.

Recent trends

The trends among other hip-hop artists in recent years vary widely. Some artists are positive and others are not. Hip-hop artists rap about many things. Some rap about what concerns them. They also tell stories. Some rappers are funny. Some try to teach important life lessons. Others are serious. Some use **profanity** (offensive words).

Sean Combs started a successful label called Bad Boy Records.

Choose wisely

Your parents, caregivers, or teachers should know what music you are listening to. They will tell you if what you are listening to is okay.

A hip-hop concert, such as this Pharrell Williams event, is exciting for fans. It is also an opportunity for an artist to spread important messages to fans, such as non-violence.

Hip-hop anniversary tour

In 2008 several hip-hop artists got together for the No Profanity Hip-Hop Anniversary Tour. Several hip-hop artists performed at different locations throughout Europe and the United States. Some of the artists who performed were Grandmaster Mele Mel, Big Daddy Kane, Afrika Bambaataa and the SoulSonic Force, and Public Enemy. The artists used the tour to tell people about No Profanity Day (9 August 2009). Their goal was for there to be no crime, violence, hate, or profanity on that day.

The beat goes on

Hip-hop music started small. From poor neighbourhoods in New York City, USA, it quickly spread all over the world. Today, major hip-hop acts are emerging from Europe. In the United Kingdom, the Streets and Dizzee Rascal (see box below) are known for their clever rhymes, while female rapper M.I.A. has political messages. In other parts of Europe, **MCs** like Bligg and Stress rap in languages other than English, including German and French.

Dizzee Rascal

Dizzee Rascal was born in London and has become a successful rapper and record **producer**. In 2003, at the age of 18, he was the youngest person ever to win the Mercury Prize for his album *Boy in da Corner*. The Mercury Prize is a yearly prize given for the best album in the UK. He raps using a "grime" style that is unique to MCs from the UK. Grime is similar to US hip-hop, but it uses faster electronic beats and even faster rhymes.

Dizzee Rascal is a popular British hip-hop artist.

As long as there is an audience for hip-hop, new stars and new styles will continue to emerge.

The future of hip-hop

Hip-hop sales have fallen by more than 40 per cent since the year 2000. Illegal copying is one reason why sales have gone down. Illegal copying is when people use a computer to copy songs and share them without paying for them. Another reason is that since 2000, audiences have become bored with the focus on violence and wealth in hip-hop.

Although hip-hop record sales have fallen over the last few years, many new hip-hop artists still record music every day. New artists are played on the radio all the time. Hip-hop will continue to develop and change with new messages and exciting new styles of music.

Timeline

1970s	New York **DJs** Afrika Bambaataa and Grandmaster Flash begin their careers. They will become stars by the early 1980s.
1973	DJ Kool Herc begins DJing parties and develops the **break beat**. This inspires **break-dancing**.
1977	The famous group of break-dancers, the Rock Steady Crew, is formed.
1979	The Sugarhill Gang releases the hip-hop hit "Rapper's Delight".
	Grandmaster Flash joins with the **MCs** known as the Furious Five.
1981	The Zulu Nation begins spreading hip-hop to Europe.
1983	Run-DMC brings MCing to the forefront of hip-hop.
1984	Rick Rubin and Russell Simmons start the hip-hop record label Def Jam.
1986	The Beastie Boys release the album *Licensed to Ill*, to **mainstream** success.
1988	Public Enemy releases the political album *It Takes a Nation of Millions to Hold Us Back*.
	N.W.A. popularizes gangsta **rap** with its first album, *Straight Outta Compton*.
1992	Death Row Records is formed and releases Dr. Dre's gangsta rap album *The Chronic*.
1994	Common releases the politically conscious album *Resurrection*.
1996	The Fugees release the popular album *The Score*.

1996	Jay-Z starts Roc-A-Fella Records and releases his first album, *Reasonable Doubt*.
1998	Lauryn Hill releases *The Miseducation of Lauryn Hill*.
1999	Dr. Dre releases *2001* and is the **producer** of Eminem's first album, *The Slim Shady LP*.
	Hip-hop becomes the top-selling type of music in the United States, with 81 million albums sold.
2000	Hip-hop album sales begin to drop.
2003	Lil Wayne begins releasing **mixtapes**.
	Dizzee Rascal's *Boy in da Corner* is released.
2004	The Streets release the album *A Grand Don't Come for Free*, which reaches number one in the UK charts.
2006	Nas is signed with Def Jam and releases the album *Hip-Hop Is Dead*.
2007	Dizzee Rascal is nominated for his second Mercury Prize award with album *Maths + English*.
2008	**Underground** hip-hop artists like Lupe Fiasco, B.o.B, Kidz in the Hall, Kid Sister, and Cool Kids begin to emerge.

Glossary

beat-boxing using the lips, mouth, tongue, and hands to sound like drums and other musical sounds

break beat extended drumbeat in a hip-hop song

break-dancing form of hip-hop dance that uses the hands and feet for exciting spin and flip movements, both standing and on the ground

culture way of life for a certain group of people

DJ short for "disc jockey", a person who plays recorded music

freestyle rapping on the spot without preparing, by using any rhymes that come to mind

funk bass-heavy musical style characterized by improvisation, horns, and strong rhythms

graffiti markings or drawings often found on buildings and pavements, usually made with spray paint

gritty displaying a hard and tough style

hustler someone who makes money through illegal or questionable ways, such as selling drugs or stealing

improvisational performing without preparing beforehand

lyrics words to a song

mainstream music that receives a lot of attention from newspapers, magazines, and television

MC short for "master of ceremonies"

mix play two records at the same time or each on their own using a switch that connects two turntables

mixtape collection of songs and freestyles usually recorded by a hip-hop artist on a CD. This CD is released on the Internet or handed out for free on the street or at a concert to promote the new hip-hop artist.

producer someone who directs the recording process and also creates music

profanity words or actions that are offensive

rap lyrics said to a rhythm, often as rhymes, by an MC in a hip-hop song. Also, the act of saying these lyrics.

rhythm in music, a rhythm is a regular beat

sample use a turntable, computer, or tape player to copy part of a song, such as a catchy beat or break

synthesizer instrument that usually resembles a keyboard and makes complex, interesting sounds

turntable record player. It uses a needle that glides across the record to make a sound.

underground music that has not become popular on television or radio, but still has many fans

urban found in or characteristic of living in a city

vandalism purposely destroying property

Find out more

Books

Dance: Hip-Hop and Urban Dance, Tamsin Fitzgerald (Heinemann Library, 2009)

Get Dancing: Street Jazz and Other Modern Dances, Rita Storey (Franklin Watts, 2005)

Hip-Hop: A Short History, Rosa Waters (Mason Crest, 2007)

Websites

A website about British hip-hop
www.britishhiphop.co.uk

A list of hip-hop music for kids can be found by using the menu on the left-hand side of this web page
www.commonsensemedia.org/music-reviews

KidzWorld's "Pioneers of Hip Hop"
www.kidzworld.com/article/5321-pioneers-of-hip-hop

Index